Coconut™

Coconut's Cookbook

Fun and Fluffy Treats to Eat

American Girl®

Published by Pleasant Company Publications
Copyright © 2004 by American Girl LLC

Questions or comments?
Call 1-800-845-0005, visit our Web site at **americangirl.com**,
or write American Girl, P.O. Box 620497, Middleton, WI 53562-0497.

Printed in China.
04 05 06 07 08 09 LEO 10 9 8 7 6 5 4 3 2 1

American Girl®, Coconut™, and the Coconut designs
and logos are trademarks of American Girl LLC.

Editorial Development: Therese Kauchak
Art Direction: Camela Decaire, Chris Lorette David
Design: Camela Decaire
Production: Kendra Pulvermacher, Mindy Rappe,
Jeannette Bailey, Judith Lary
Styling: Sarajane Lien
Illustrations: Casey Lukatz

Welcome, chefs!

All the recipes in this cookbook—from
an all-white sundae to a fluffy fruit dip to
fun toppings for your popcorn—are inspired
by an American Girl's best friend, Coconut.
You'll even learn how to decorate a cake with
an image of Coconut's face. Make a treat
for yourself or to share with a friend.

Don't wait. Dig in!

Your friends at American Girl

Cream Soda Float

This sweet sipper is sure to float your boat.

For each float, you will need:
- 2 scoops vanilla ice cream
- 1 can cream soda
- 1 cookie

Put the scoops of vanilla ice cream into a tall glass. Fill the rest of the glass with cream soda. Add a tall spoon or straw, and garnish with a cookie.

Snowball Marshmallows

Make marshmallow sweets that melt in your mouth.

For each treat, you will need:
- 3 marshmallows
- 1 bamboo skewer
- chocolate Magic Shell topping
- sprinkles
- wax paper
- cookie sheet

Carefully slide a bamboo skewer through 3 marshmallows. Place the skewer on a cookie sheet and freeze until firm, about ½ hour. Hold the skewer over a sheet of wax paper and, from the side, drizzle the tops of the marshmallows with chocolate Magic Shell topping. Turn the skewer slowly to cover the marshmallow tops all the way around. Add sprinkles, set on a cookie sheet covered with wax paper, and refreeze until ready to serve.

Almond Toasty

This warm drink is perfect for sipping on a chilly day.

For each serving, you will need:
- 1 mug of milk
- 2 tablespoons sugar
- 1 drop almond extract
- mini marshmallows

♥ Ask an adult to help you warm a mugful of milk in the microwave on high for 1 minute 45 seconds, stirring halfway through. Add 2 tablespoons sugar and a drop of almond extract. Top with mini marshmallows and stir gently.

Fruit Fluff

Whip up a dip that's delicious for fruit.

You will need:
- 8 ounces cream cheese
- 7 ounces marshmallow creme
- favorite fruits in bite-size pieces
- plastic party skewers or toothpicks

In a bowl, combine one 8-ounce package softened cream cheese and one 7-ounce jar marshmallow creme. Stir well. Using party skewers or toothpicks, pick your favorite fruits and dip in.

Very Cool Cupcakes

Ice cream cupcakes are perfect for decorating.

You will need:
- vanilla ice cream
- paper cupcake liners
- muffin tin
- decorator icing
- sprinkles
- sugars
- candies

Let ice cream soften for about 30 minutes. Place cupcake liners in a muffin tin. Spoon softened ice cream into liners. Freeze until solid.

Decorate with colored decorator icing, sprinkles, sugars, and candies. Tip: Plan topping ideas before removing the cupcakes from the freezer, so they don't melt too quickly while you're decorating.

All-White Sundae

Make an ice cream sundae that's as white as snow.

For each sundae, you will need:
- vanilla ice cream
- white chocolate chips
- marshmallow creme
- whipped cream
- white sprinkles
- white candy

In a bowl or sundae glass, layer white chocolate chips between scoops of vanilla ice cream. Top with marshmallow creme, whipped cream, and sprinkles. Finish with a piece of white candy.

Perfect Parfait

If you like cheesecake, you'll like this parfait.

You will need:
- 8 ounces cream cheese
- 6 tablespoons powdered sugar
- 1 cup whipped topping
- 1 teaspoon lemon juice
- blueberries
- strawberries
- Fruit Roll-Ups

In a large bowl, mix 8 ounces softened cream cheese and 6 tablespoons powdered sugar with a fork or whisk until fluffy. Add 1 cup whipped topping and 1 teaspoon lemon juice. Stir until smooth. Layer cream cheese mixture in glasses with blueberries and sliced strawberries. Top with whipped topping and stars cut from Fruit Roll-Ups.

Flurry Floatsicles

This pop tastes grape!

For each pop, you will need:
- vanilla ice cream
- grape juice
- 3-ounce paper cup
- food-safe stick
- foil

Scoop vanilla ice cream into a
3-ounce paper cup, filling the cup
about ⅓ full. Press the ice cream
firmly into the bottom of the cup.
Insert a food-safe stick into ice cream.
Slowly pour grape juice into the cup
until it is almost full. Cover the top of
the cup with foil, poking the end of the
stick through the foil. Freeze until firm.

Popcorn Toppers

Pick a popcorn topper that pops your top!

You will need:
- warm popcorn
- your choice of toppings

Add the ingredients below to a bag of hot buttered microwave popcorn. Then shake and share.

Peanut Butter Cup:
½ cup chocolate chips, ½ cup peanut butter chips

Cheese, Please:
2 tablespoons powdered cheese topping

Cinnamon Twist:
¼ cup sugar, ½ teaspoon cinnamon

Pucker Popper:
1 teaspoon dry ranch dressing mix

Movie Madness:
1 cup Milk Duds

Texas Two-Step:
1 teaspoon taco seasoning, 2 table-spoons powdered cheese topping

Tip: Dip the melon baller in warm water
between scoops to make scooping easier.

Ice Cream Balls

Try several flavors of ice cream for an eye-catching treat.

You will need:
- ice cream
- melon-baller scoop
- wax paper
- cookie sheet
- plastic wrap
- coconut, sprinkles, nonpareils, and other toppings

Pour a variety of toppings into separate small bowls. Set two spoons by the toppings. Use a melon baller to scoop out a small ball of ice cream. Drop the ball into the topping of your choice, and toss it gently with the spoons to coat. Set the ice cream ball on a cookie sheet covered with wax paper. Working quickly, repeat until you have as many balls as you want. Cover the cookie sheet with plastic wrap and refreeze.

Tiny Tarts

Mini yogurt pies are a breeze to freeze and fun to decorate.

You will need:
- small premade tart crusts
- whipped topping
- flavored yogurt
- candies, coconut, or other toppings

You'll find tiny tart crusts near the pie supplies in grocery stores. Mix together equal amounts of whipped topping and cold yogurt—vanilla or fruit yogurt works well. Pour into tart shells. Freeze for 1 hour. Decorate the tarts with candies, coconut, or other delights.

Bug Bite Cookies

Invent a bug, then eat it!

You will need:
- marshmallow puff cookies or snack cakes
- licorice string
- candy buttons
- cake decorations
- frosting

Decorate marshmallow puff cookies or snack cakes to look like crawly creatures. Use licorice for antennae and cake decorations and candy buttons for eyes. Stick on the candy with dabs of frosting.

Daisy Cake

Top your favorite cake with marshmallow daisies.

You will need:
- 1 cake, baked and cooled
- yellow food coloring
- vanilla frosting
- scissors or kitchen shears
- mini marshmallows
- yellow decorator icing in tube

♥ Using a boxed mix or your favorite recipe, have an adult help you bake a cake. Let it cool. Add a few drops of yellow food coloring to vanilla frosting, and mix until color is even throughout. Ice cake with yellow frosting. Wash the scissors and dry them. Snip each marshmallow into 3 slices. For each daisy, carefully press 5 marshmallow slices into the frosting to look like petals. Fill the center with a dab of yellow decorator icing.

Coconut Face Cake

Top off a brownie cake with Coconut's image!

You will need:
- 1 package brownie mix
- 7-inch cake pan
- powdered sugar
- fine-mesh strainer
- Coconut template in the back of this book

Follow the recipe on the package for cake-like brownies. Ask an adult to turn the cake out of the pan upside down. Place the Coconut template on top. Cover the remaining cake surface with paper towels. Fill strainer with confectioners' sugar. Gently shake strainer over stencil to dust sugar lightly and evenly over the top. Carefully lift off the template and towels. *Voilà!*

Recipe for Fun!

Make your own recipe cards!

These Coconut recipe cards can be popped out for easy use. Use them for your favorite recipes, or send cards to the chefs in your family and collect their favorites.